Forests

by Michelle Hyde Parsons

Table of Contents

Introduction 2
Chapter 1 What Are Forests? 4
Chapter 2 Why Are Forests Important? 8
Chapter 3 What Harms Forests? 12
Chapter 4 How Can We Save Forests? 16
Summary 20
Glossary 22
Index 24

Introduction

Forests are important to people. Read to learn about forests.

Words to Know

acid rain

animals

forests

habitats

oxygen

plants

recycle

trees

See the Glossary on page 22.

Chapter 1

What Are Forests?

Forests have **trees**. Different trees grow in forests.

It's A Fact

Some trees lose their leaves in winter. Some trees have needles. The needles stay on the trees all winter.

▲ Trees grow in forests.

Forests have **plants**. Different plants grow in forests. Large plants grow in forests. Small plants grow in forests.

▲ This plant grows in the rain forest.

▲ This plant grows in the cloud forest.

Chapter 1

Forests have **animals**. Different animals live in forests.

▲ Gorillas live in this forest. The forest is in Africa.

What Are Forests?

Large animals live in forests. Small animals live in forests.

▲ The beetle lives in this forest. The forest is in North America.

Try This

Forest Animals

Work with a partner.
1. Choose a continent.
2. Read about forests on that continent.
3. Read about animals in the forests.
4. Make a list of the animals.
5. Draw pictures of the animals.

▲ The Great Blue Heron lives in this forest. The forest is in North America.

Chapter 2

Why Are Forests Important?

Forests are important for animals. Animals find food in forests.

▲ Squirrels find nuts in forests. Nuts grow on trees.

Forests have homes for animals. Forests are **habitats** for animals.

▲ Some raccoons live in forests.

It's A Fact

Rain forests are hot, wet forests. Rain forests are on many continents. Many different animals live in rain forests. This chart lists some animals.

Continent	Animals
Africa	chimpanzees, parrots
Asia	orangutans, tigers
Australia	koalas, cockatoos
South America	monkeys, jaguars

Chapter 2

Forests are important for people. Trees and plants make **oxygen**. People need oxygen to live.

▲ People breathe oxygen.

Why Are Forests Important?

People use wood from forests. People use wood to make things.

▲ People use wood.

Chapter 3

What Harms Forests?

Fires harm forests. Fires burn trees and plants. The trees and plants die.

▲ Forest fires harm forests.

Fires burn animals. The animals die.

Did You Know?

Smokey Bear is a symbol of fire safety.

Chapter 3

Acid rain harms forests. Acid rain kills trees.

▲ Acid rain killed this forest.

Did You Know?

Cars cause acid rain.

What Harms Forests?

People harm forests. People cut down too many trees.

▲ People cut down forests.

Chapter 4

How Can We Save Forests?

People can be careful with camp fires.
People can put out camp fires.

It's A Fact
Camp fires can cause forest fires.

▲ People make camp fires.

People can stop acid rain. More people can walk. More people can ride buses. More people can ride trains.

▲ People ride buses.

Chapter 4

People can **recycle**. People can recycle paper. Paper is made from wood. Paper is made from trees.

▲ People can recycle paper.

Solve This

One ton of paper uses 20 trees. How many trees do 4,000 pounds of paper use? (Hint: One ton = 2,000 pounds)

Answer: 40 trees

How Can We Save Forests?

People can plant new forests.

▲ People can plant new trees.

Summary

Forests have trees and plants. Forests have animals. Forests are important for animals and people.

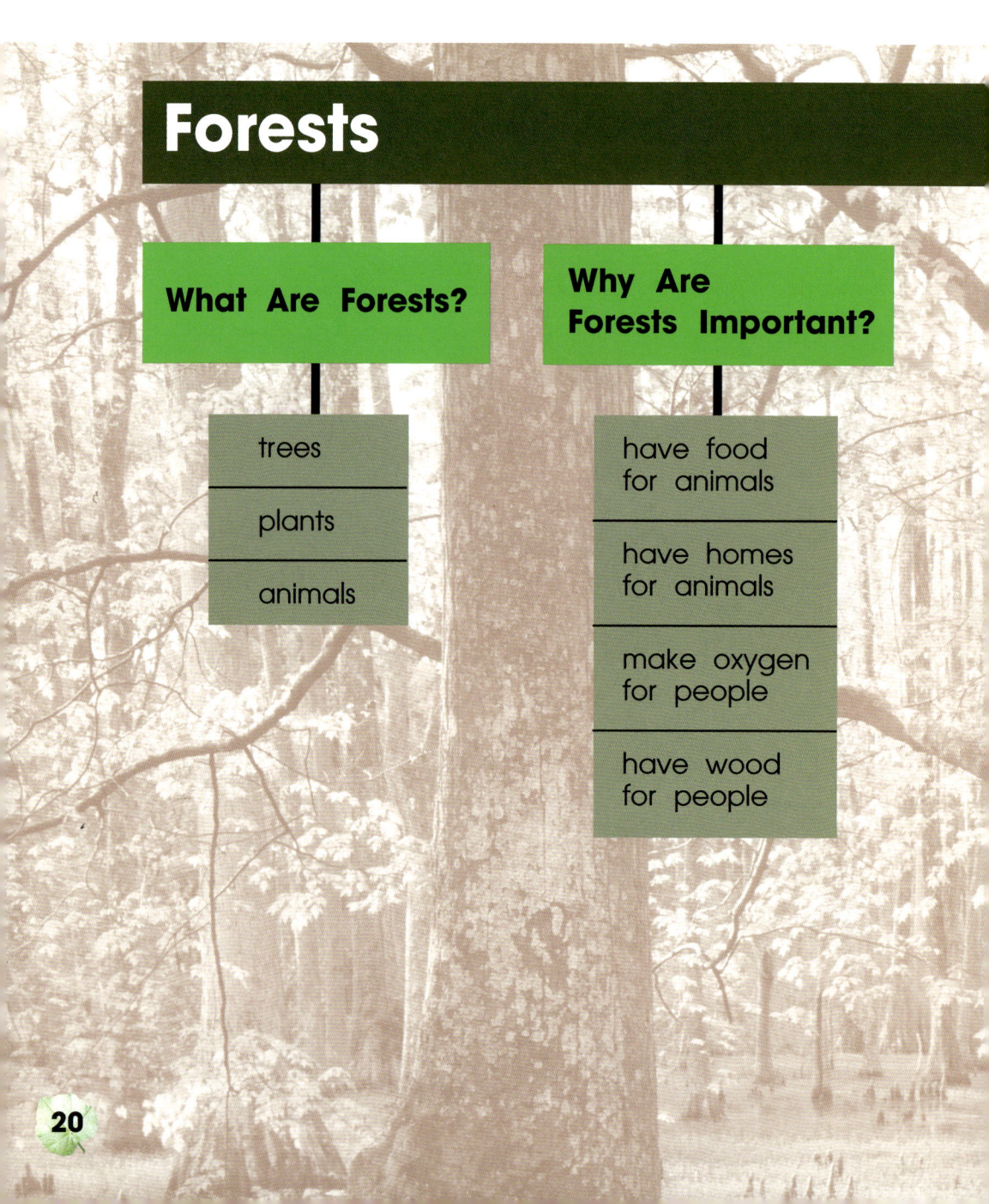

Forests

What Are Forests?
- trees
- plants
- animals

Why Are Forests Important?
- have food for animals
- have homes for animals
- make oxygen for people
- have wood for people

Forest fires harm forests. Acid rain harms forests. People can do many things to save forests.

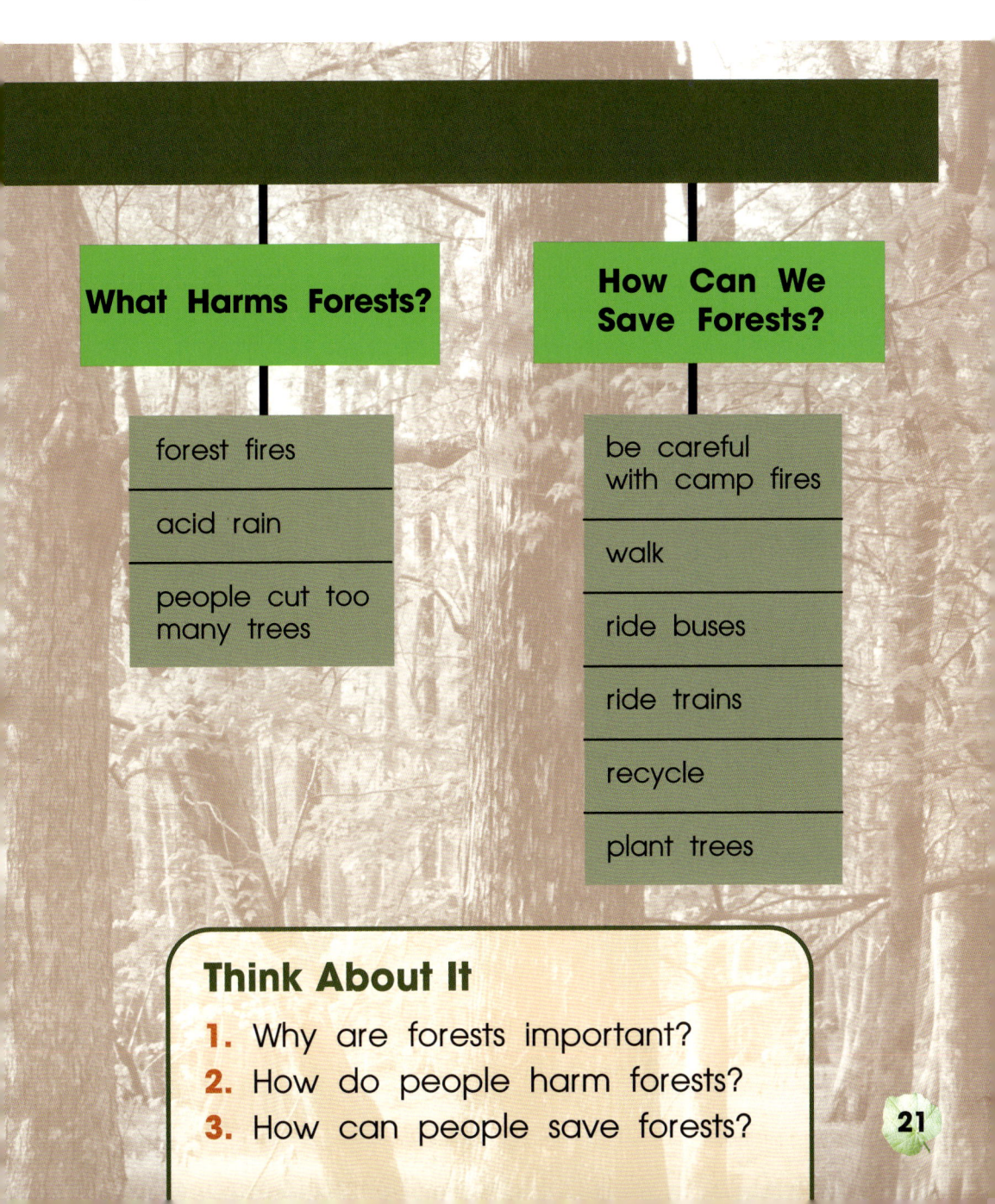

What Harms Forests?	How Can We Save Forests?
forest fires	be careful with camp fires
acid rain	walk
people cut too many trees	ride buses
	ride trains
	recycle
	plant trees

Think About It

1. Why are forests important?
2. How do people harm forests?
3. How can people save forests?

Glossary

acid rain rain that has poisons

Acid rain can kill forests.

animals living things that can move

Animals live in forests.

forests large areas of trees

Forests have trees and plants.

habitats places where animals or people live

Forests are **habitats** for many animals.

oxygen a gas with no color and no odor

People breathe **oxygen**.

plants living things that cannot move

Plants grow in forests.

recycle use again

People **recycle** paper.

trees woody plants

Trees grow in forests.

Index

acid rain, 14, 17, 21

animals, 6-9, 13, 20

fires, 12-13, 16, 21

food, 8, 20

forests, 2-12, 14-16, 19-21

habitats, 9

oxygen, 10, 20

plants, 5, 10, 12, 20

recycle, 18, 21

trees, 4, 10, 12, 14-15, 18-21

wood, 11, 18, 20